It's a Dad's Thing

PART 1 - THE STUPID DAD

ADAM ATCHA

Balboa Press books may be ordered through booksellers or by contacting:

Balboa Press
A Division of Hay House
1663 Liberty Drive
Bloomington, IN 47403
www.balboapress.com.au
AU TFN: 1 800 844 925 (Toll Free inside Australia)
AU Local: 0283 107 086 (+61 2 8310 7086 from outside Australia)

ISBN: 978-1-5043-2293-5 (sc)
ISBN: 978-1-5043-2294-2 (e)

Print information available on the last page.

Balboa Press rev. date: 10/21/2020

BALBOA PRESS
A DIVISION OF HAY HOUSE

A loveless Dad loves you for
who you are and hurts himself,

A Ruthless Dad loves
you differently

A Daddy's girl is a Princess

A loving Dad loves you and
himself unconditionally

A forgiving Dad hates
himself and Loves you

A Dad with a Pure love
sees and hears no Evil but
knows everything yet does
not want to Hate you

A Dad in Love speaks nothing
but his Offspring's –

A Faithful Dad loves
nobody but her –

– A Bisexual Dad becomes
better than a Heterosexual dad

A Dad love who hates himself
can only love Her more than
Anybody in the world

A Gay dad is Insecure to be a
better Role Model than most

JUSTIFY IF NOT
TRUE – Correspondence
A. ATCHA 0466571899

A Racist Dad makes Her
superior to Most Differently

An Aggressive Dad is
Overprotective and Lawful –

We are all Dads who need
Love as Women do!

Our insecurities out smart
any Women as them —

We Fall In Love with our
Daughters Naturally with
no explanation – Why
Who and When

As Dads we Love ourselves
through the Effort we put into
our Relations with Her or Him

A Highly sophisticated Dad wants
everything in order to Love you.

A Snob Dad wants to impress
others through Great Family
Values and Authority

Printed in the United States
By Bookmasters